A MEMORIAL FOR MR. LINCOLN

A MEMORIAL FOR

Brent Ashabranner

**Photographs by Jennifer Ashabranner
and historical photographs**

G. P. PUTNAM'S SONS
New York

MR. LINCOLN

Text copyright © 1992 by Brent Ashabranner.
Photographs copyright © 1992 by Jennifer Ashabranner.

G. P. Putnam's Sons, a division of The Putnam & Grosset Group,
200 Madison Avenue, New York, NY 10016.
Published simultaneously in Canada.
Printed in the United States of America.

Book design by Joy Taylor

Library of Congress Cataloging-in-Publication Data
Ashabranner, Brent K., 1921–
    A memorial for Mr. Lincoln / Brent Ashabranner : photographs by Jennifer Ashabranner.
        p.   cm.
    Includes bibliographical references (p. 103) and index.
    Summary: Briefly discusses Lincoln's role in American history and describes the planning and building of the monument dedicated to his memory in 1922.
    1. Lincoln Memorial (Washington, D.C.)—Juvenile literature. 2. Lincoln, Abraham, 1809–1865—Monuments—Washington (D.C.)—Juvenile literature. 3. Washington (D.C.)—Buildings, structures, etc.—Juvenile literature. [1. Lincoln Memorial (Washington, D.C.)] I. Ashabranner, Jennifer, ill. II. Title.
F203.4.L73A84   1992
973.7'092—dc20   91-40249
                                                                                        CIP–
                                                                                         AC

ISBN 0-399-22273-1

10 9 8 7 6 5 4 3 2 1
First Impression

THIS BOOK IS FOR

Olivia-Jené Fagon

Contents

A MEMORIAL FOR MR. LINCOLN

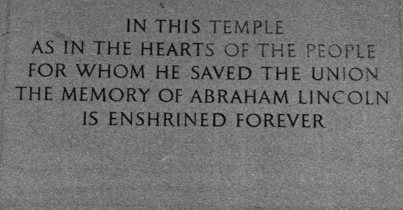

IN THIS TEMPLE
AS IN THE HEARTS OF THE PEOPLE
FOR WHOM HE SAVED THE UNION
THE MEMORY OF ABRAHAM LINCOLN
IS ENSHRINED FOREVER

ONE

In This Temple

THE HIGH school choral group from Sumter, South Carolina, started its concert on the reflecting pool terrace in front of the Lincoln Memorial. They sang such ear-catching songs as "You Are the Wind Beneath My Wings" and "Love Changes Everything," and visitors to the memorial that August day paused to listen and applaud. Some of the ice cream and hot dog vendors stopped working and drifted over, which was unusual. The Sumter singers then climbed the great sweep of steps leading to the memorial and closed with "America" and waved American flags as they sang a rousing "God Bless the U.S.A."

Hundreds of school groups visit the Lincoln Memorial each spring and summer as part of field trips to Washington, D.C. Some of them arrange with the National Park Service to give an open-air concert at the memorial just to add a special memory to their visit. During the summer I had watched a number of school bands and choral groups from all over the

The Sumter High School Show Choir, Sumter, South Carolina, on the terrace in front of the Lincoln Memorial.

country perform at the Lincoln Memorial. Most had done well, but none better than the Sumter Show Choir.

I talked to Sonja Sepulveda, the faculty musical director at Sumter High School. "We call it a show choir because they both sing and dance," she explained. She told me the students raised money for their field trip by selling magazine subscriptions, having turkey and cheese cake sales, and washing cars. "The parents pitch in and help."

As good as they were, the Sumter Show Choir had first caught my attention because of where they were from. The first shots of the Civil War were fired at Fort Sumter. The fort and the town of Sumter are not the same, of course; but they are both in South Carolina, and South Carolina was the first state to secede from the Union in 1861. Now, 125 years after the Civil War, these students from a South Carolina high school came to sing patriotic songs on the steps of the memorial to the man who saved the Union. Their presence seemed to symbolize how much the Lincoln Memorial belongs to the whole country.

"We came to Washington mainly to give a concert at the National Cathedral," Sonja said. "At the last minute we were asked if we wanted to put on a show at the Lincoln Memorial, too. That was about three hours before our National Cathedral performance, and I wondered if we should do it. But the whole choir wanted to do the extra show. Shaw Air Force Base is near Sumter, and some of the students in the choir have dads who were in Desert Storm. The kids wanted to wave the flag on the steps of the Lincoln Memorial."

IN THE YEARS since its dedication in 1922, the Lincoln Memorial has become America's most revered national monument. The best estimates are that over 150 million visitors have climbed the wide marble steps of the memorial and entered the great

Lost in thought. A young serviceman reads Lincoln's Second Inaugural Address engraved on the north wall of the Memorial.

chamber. On my many trips to the memorial, the crowds were sometimes huge. Even at midnight or five o'clock in the morning, I was not the only visitor. The Lincoln Memorial is never closed.

For most people a visit to the memorial is a once-in-a-lifetime experience, a chance to gaze up at Lincoln's serious yet kindly face, to have one's picture taken in front of the colossal statue, to read the immortal words of the Gettysburg Address and the Second Inaugural Address engraved on the south and north walls, to drink in the incomparable view of the Washington Monument and Capitol beyond the long reflecting pool, to walk to the west side of the memorial and look across the Potomac River at Robert E. Lee's home, now itself a shrine, standing on a high hill in Arlington National Cemetery. The very heart of American history is here.

Many important and famous people, not only Americans but dignitaries from all over the world, go to the Lincoln Memorial every year to take part in ceremonies or to pay the respects of their government. For some American presidents the Lincoln Memorial clearly has had special meaning. Despite the burdens of the Great Depression and the Second World War, Franklin D. Roosevelt always found time to visit the memorial every year on February 12, sometimes in bitterly cold weather, for the commemoration of Lincoln's birthday. On his early-morning walks, President Harry Truman would sometimes drop by the Lincoln Memorial. Flanked by his Secret Service walking companions, Truman would climb the memorial steps and chat with the rangers on duty or say a cheery good morning to some early visitor startled to be suddenly face-to-face with the president of the United States.

But it is the ordinary people, the kind of people Abraham Lincoln loved and respected, who have taken his memorial to their hearts. They are awed by its beauty but not intimidated by its grandeur. For all its magnificence, Americans have found

the Lincoln Memorial to be a warm and friendly place. Perhaps it is the figure of Lincoln himself, so real, so unthreatening despite his great size and his massive chair, almost like a throne, yet not a throne. Perhaps it is the knowledge most Americans have of who this man was and what he believed in.

To see the great words carved in stone is to *feel* them in a new way:

With malice toward none, with charity for all . . .

. . . that government of the people, by the people,
for the people shall not perish from the earth.

The Park rangers, usually three on duty during the day, two or three at night, add to the feeling of friendliness and warmth. They are in uniform, and they are responsible for the well-being of the memorial; but they are not so much guards as they are men and women who have absorbed the spirit of this very special place, have learned its history, and love to talk about it with visitors and answer their questions. There is no guided tour of the Lincoln Memorial and no audiotaped story of its history to listen to by pushing a button. But Ranger James Woolsey will answer your questions about the murals on the north and south walls, explaining that they symbolize Lincoln's two greatest achievements: saving the Union and freeing the slaves. In the evening when the city lights have come on, Ranger Nelson Marks will take you to a spot on the north side of the memorial where you can get one of the most beautiful views of Washington. Ranger Bruce Stocking will happily share with you his knowledge of how the memorial was built and of the materials that went into its building. And if you tell Ranger Mike Moreno there is a pigeon with a broken leg at the back of the memorial or an injured duck in the reflecting pool, Mike

*Probably the most popular place in Washington to pose
for a picture is in front of Lincoln's statue.*

A pigeon finds Lincoln's relaxed right hand a more comfortable land-ing place than his clenched left fist. Rangers wage a friendly but in-conclusive war with pigeons in the Lincoln Memorial.

At left, David Rowen and Cathy Callen from San Jose, California, talk with Rangers James Woolsey (left) and Victor Leyva.

will try to find the unfortunate bird and take care of it. Working at the memorial is far more than just a job.

On spring and summer nights crowds are drawn to the memorial as moths are drawn to a flame. Lights make dramatic silhouettes of the soaring marble columns. Lincoln changes, too, as the sun disappears and only artificial light falls on him. Does he seem more lonely? Is there a greater sense that he is watching over all who are there? Perhaps that is why some people seem reluctant to leave, even as the night grows older. Perhaps that is why small groups of young men and women, high school students mostly, sit on the memorial steps, talking quietly, laughing quietly, watching the fireflies glowing in the surrounding shadows.

When finally the time comes to leave, most visitors turn for a last look at Lincoln, and they read again the words above his head:

IN THIS TEMPLE

AS IN THE HEARTS OF THE PEOPLE

FOR WHOM HE SAVED THE UNION

THE MEMORY OF ABRAHAM LINCOLN

IS ENSHRINED FOREVER

Those words, written by Royal Cortissoz, were first submitted to the Lincoln Memorial Commission for approval. A number of attempts were made to write a better inscription. Chief Justice of the Supreme Court William Howard Taft was one of those who tried. At that time he was also chairman of the Lincoln Memorial Commission. Finally he gave up, saying he could not imagine what had given him the idea he could improve the words.

Millions who have read the inscription would agree with Chief Justice Taft. The words need no improving.

❧ TWO

With Malice toward None

H<small>IS WORK</small> was so colossal, in the face of such discouragement, that none will dispute that he was incomparably the greatest of our Presidents."

Thus did President Warren G. Harding assess Abraham Lincoln at the dedication of the Lincoln Memorial in 1922; although George Washington was "the father of our country" and Franklin D. Roosevelt brought us through the Great Depression and the years of World War II, most Americans would agree with Harding. It was Lincoln's fate to preserve the Union and to become the Great Emancipator. Greatness aside, few Americans would disagree that Lincoln was and remains our most loved president whose life, deeds, and words have soaked into the bone and sinew of our country.

Born in a log cabin in the most humble circumstances, Lincoln as a boy worked on his father's farm, had youthful adventures on a Mississippi River raft, read books by firelight to educate himself, became a successful lawyer, and rose to the

This photograph of President Abraham Lincoln was taken by Civil War photographer Matthew Brady in 1864.

highest office in the land. That personal history in itself was the raw material of myth and a story of the American dream in its purest form.

But the heart of the story was yet to come. It was Lincoln's destiny as president to save the Union from dismemberment in a terrible civil war and to end the nation's ugly blight of slavery. He accomplished those enormous tasks by demonstrating throughout his presidency the patience, understanding, courage to believe in himself, and good common sense that were at least in part products of his frontier life and his native intelligence.

Lincoln never left any doubt about what he thought of the practice of some human beings enslaving other human beings. "He who would *be* no slave, must consent to *have* no slave," Lincoln wrote in a letter to H. L. Pierce in 1859. "Those who deny freedom to others, deserve it not for themselves; and, under a just God, cannot long retain it."

He called slavery a "monstrous injustice" and declared that in "giving freedom to the slave, we *assure* freedom to the *free.*"

Lincoln believed that the founding fathers intended the Declaration of Independence to apply to all people, not just those of the white race. "They did not mean to say that all were equal in color, size, intellect, moral development, or social capacity," he said in a speech in 1857. "They defined with tolerable distinctness, in what respects they did consider all men created equal—equal in 'certain inalienable Rights, among which are Life, Liberty, and the Pursuit of Happiness.' This they said, and this they meant."

With one brilliant metaphor adapted from the Bible, Lincoln described what he believed would be the eventual effect of slavery on the United States: "A house divided against itself cannot stand. I believe this government cannot endure permanently half slave and half free." And in words that could not

13

be clearer, he said, "If slavery is not wrong, nothing is wrong."

But from his first day in the White House, Lincoln knew clearly what his primary task was to be. He was personally, morally opposed to slavery, but his duty as president was to preserve the Union. If a minority was permitted to set up a separate government whenever it disagreed with the majority, the whole concept of Union quickly would become meaningless.

The South feared that upon becoming president, Lincoln would immediately try to make the owning of slaves illegal. To no avail Lincoln tried to make clear that his policy would first be to attempt to prevent the spread of slavery to new territories and then find ways to compensate slave owners who freed their slaves. Unconvinced, South Carolina seceded from the Union on December 20, 1860, even before Lincoln became president. Six other Southern states quickly followed and with South Carolina formed the Confederate States of America. Five weeks after Lincoln took the oath of office as president on March 4, 1861, Confederate guns fired on the federal station of Fort Sumter in Charleston Harbor, South Carolina, and the Civil War had begun. Four other Southern states seceded, forming an eleven-state Confederacy.

Northern abolitionists clamored for the immediate freeing of all slaves by total war if necessary. Others in the North advocated letting the Southern states go their separate way rather than wage war to keep them in the Union. In his famous open letter to Horace Greeley, editor of the *New York Tribune,* in August 1862, Lincoln answered both the abolitionists and those who would condone secession.

"My paramount object in this struggle is to save the Union, and is not either to save or to destroy slavery," the president wrote. "What I do about slavery and the colored race, I do because I believe it helps to save the Union."

By the fall of 1862, early Confederate victories on Virginia

IN THIS TEMPLE
AS IN THE HEARTS OF THE PEOPLE
FOR WHOM HE SAVED THE UNION
THE MEMORY OF ABRAHAM LINCOLN
IS ENSHRINED FOREVER

The inscription above Lincoln's statue was written by Royal Cortis-soz, who served for fifty years as art critic of the **New York Tribune.** *Cortissoz and Henry Bacon were friends of long standing, both having worked early in their careers in the architectural offices of McKim, Mead, and White. Cortissoz wrote the Lincoln Memorial inscription at Bacon's suggestion. Although Cortissoz was the author of many highly regarded biographies and books of art criticism, he always said that he was proudest of the one-sentence inscription carved in stone above Lincoln's statue.*

battlefields—at Bull Run, on the York Peninsula, in the Shenandoah Valley—together with growing Northern demoralization convinced Lincoln that the only way to defeat the Confederacy was to abolish slavery in the rebellious states. This he did by executive order in September 1862, and with the formal Emancipation Proclamation on January 1, 1863.

The immediate effect of the Emancipation Proclamation was to give the North a new sense of purpose in fighting the war; now the war was not only to restore the Union but to restore a Union that would be free of the moral disgrace of slavery. The Proclamation also created increased support for the Union cause in European countries, particularly Great Britain. While the Proclamation could be enforced in the rebellious states only with Union military success, the ultimate effect as the war progressed was to deplete the Confederacy manpower reserve and add to the fighting forces of the Union. By the end of the war, almost two hundred thousand black soldiers—many of them newly freed slaves—had been enlisted in Northern armies.

With the signing of the Emancipation Proclamation, Lincoln shifted his philosophical position. No longer did he believe that restoring the Union under any conditions was sufficient. The restored Union had to be a new nation that had rid itself of the sin of slavery. Lincoln's most powerful statement of his belief found expression in his Second Inaugural Address as he began his second term as president in 1865.

Speaking of the North and South, he said, "Both read the same Bible and pray to the same God, and each invokes His aid against the other. It may seem strange that any men should dare to ask a just God's assistance in wringing their bread from the sweat of other men's faces, but let us judge not that we be not judged."

And later in his short address Lincoln said, "Fondly do we hope—fervently do we pray—that this mighty scourge of war

WITH MALICE TOWARD NONE WITH CHARITY
FOR ALL WITH FIRMNESS IN THE RIGHT AS
GOD GIVES US TO SEE THE RIGHT LET US
STRIVE ON TO FINISH THE WORK WE ARE IN
TO BIND UP THE NATION'S WOUNDS TO CARE
FOR HIM WHO SHALL HAVE BORNE THE BAT-
TLE AND FOR HIS WIDOW AND HIS ORPHAN-
TO DO ALL WHICH MAY ACHIEVE AND CHER-
ISH A JUST AND LASTING PEACE AMONG
OURSELVES AND WITH ALL NATIONS ·

may speedily pass away. Yet if God wills that it continue until all the wealth piled by the bondsman's two hundred and fifty years of unrequited toil shall be sunk and until every drop of blood drawn with the lash shall be paid by another drawn with the sword, as was said three thousand years ago so still it must be said, 'the judgments of the Lord are true and righteous altogether.'"

The president's message was clear: No matter what the cost, the war would continue until every slave had been freed. But in his concluding words Lincoln extended the hand of brotherhood to the South: "With malice toward none, with charity for all . . . let us bind up the nation's wounds." To the North he was saying the government would wage a hard war to preserve the Union and free the slaves; to the South he was saying the government would be as understanding as it could be in bringing the seceding states back into the Union.

Lincoln knew that the Emancipation Proclamation would in time have to be supported by a constitutional amendment that would make slavery illegal not only in the rebellious states but in every state in the Union. He worked hard for such an amendment—the Thirteenth Amendment to the Constitution—which was passed by the House of Representatives in January 1865, and ratified, or approved, later that year.

Not only did Lincoln bear the heaviest burdens of any American president, he was beset throughout his years of leadership by problems of finding competent military commanders, by a critical and highly uncooperative Congress, by a cabinet divided by internal hatred, and by a national press that assailed him as no leader has been assailed before or since. Angry editorials called him a tyrant, a stupid bungler in military affairs, a coward, a hick. He was made to look ridiculous in newspaper and magazine cartoons. Lincoln was hurt by these attacks, but they did not shake his faith in the rightness of his decisions. In the darkest days of the war, when the outcome was perilously in doubt, he wrote these words, which were found among his papers after his death:

> If I were trying to read, much less answer all the attacks made on me, this shop might as well be closed for business. I do the best I know how, the very best I can; and I mean to keep on doing it to the end. If the end brings me out all right, what is said against me will not amount to anything. If the end brings me out all wrong, ten angels swearing I was right would make no difference.

By early 1865 Lincoln knew that the end was going to bring him out all right. Slowly the Union armies had ground down those of the Confederacy. On a quiet Sunday, the ninth of April, Robert E. Lee, general-in-chief of all Confederate armies, surrendered the Army of Northern Virginia to Ulysses S. Grant at Appomattox Courthouse. The terrible Civil War that had taken almost half a million lives from the North and South was effectively over. The states would be one Union again.

Slavery had been abolished in the South, and a constitutional amendment would soon make the owning of human beings by other human beings a crime in every state. Many of the president's severest critics were beginning to change their minds about him.

This man who had borne the nation's tragedy on his shoulders and its sorrow in his heart, who had suffered the personal tragedy of a beloved son's death in the White House, knew a measure of peace at last. In one of his books about Lincoln, John Nicolay, one of Lincoln's two confidential secretaries, told of a talk that the president had with his wife during a carriage ride on Good Friday afternoon, April 14.

"Mary," he said, "we have had a hard time of it since we came to Washington, but the war is over, and with God's blessing we may hope for four years of peace and happiness, and then we will go back to Illinois and pass the rest of our lives in quiet."

That night while enjoying a performance of a comedy, *Our American Cousin*, at Ford's Theater a few blocks from the White House, Lincoln was shot by John Wilkes Booth. He died the next morning at twenty-two minutes past seven without regaining consciousness.

The country awakened that morning to news telegraphed from Washington that it could scarcely believe. The president had been assassinated. The grave, gentle, courageous man who had led the nation through four years of bitter war lay dead at the moment of rejoicing over victory. People were stunned. Many refused to believe what they heard or read. In every city they gathered in huge, silent crowds in front of newspaper offices and telegraph offices to wait for the latest word. People gathered in Southern cities also because they knew that the South's best hope of a humane reconstruction period after the war had rested with Lincoln.

Indignation meetings followed, with speakers calling for

A Currier and Ives print, depicting the assassination of President Lincoln by John Wilkes Booth.

revenge against the assassins and against Southern leaders presumed to be a part of the assassination plot. But overwhelmingly the emotion was grief. The president's murder shocked people everywhere into a sudden realization of what the nation had lost. Lincoln had led them through four years of bitter, deadly conflict. They remembered his gaunt, sad face. They remembered the way he had held the Union steadily on course. They remembered his clear and simple words at Gettysburg that made them understand why they had to endure and prevail in such a cruel civil war. In the few hours between the fatal

20

shot on Good Friday and the coming of Easter Sunday, the seeds of Abraham Lincoln as man, myth, and American folk hero took root forever.

On Monday evening Lincoln's embalmed body was placed in a large coffin and carried to the East Room of the White House. A huge catafalque—a structure for holding a coffin during elaborate state funerals—had been built in the East Room, and Lincoln's coffin was placed on it. Four eleven-foot poles at the corners of the catafalque supported an arched canopy. The finest black velvet and crepe together with black satin rosettes decorated the catafalque.

On Tuesday the White House was opened so that the people could pay their last respects and have a final glimpse of the fallen leader. When the west driveway gate of the White House was opened at nine-thirty that morning, a line with five to six people abreast already extended for over a mile. For eight hours, tens of thousands of men, women, and children filed past the coffin in the East Room, pausing for not more than a few seconds to look down at Lincoln's face.

Wednesday morning the funeral was held in the East Room. Invitations were severely limited, but still over six hundred persons were jammed into the room. General Grant was there as was former Vice President Andrew Johnson, now in but his fifth day as president. Cabinet members, Supreme Court justices, prominent members of Congress, state governors who had been able to reach Washington in time were all there. At the foot of the coffin sat Robert, the Lincolns' twenty-two-year-old son. With him were other members of the Lincoln family, but Mary Todd Lincoln was not present. The president's wife spent the entire day in her room, too emotionally distraught to attend the funeral or any of the other ceremonies.

At exactly ten minutes past noon the funeral service began. Four ministers, including the chaplain of the Senate, participated; Dr. Phineas Densmore Gurney, pastor of the

Two participants in Civil War–era dress pose in front of the statue of the Great Emancipator at the commemoration of his 182nd birthday, February 12, 1991.

Presbyterian Church in Washington that Lincoln had attended, gave the funeral sermon. At that same hour throughout the United States and in Canada, twenty-five million people gathered in their local churches to hear funeral sermons and to pray together.

After the funeral ceremonies in the East Room, the solemn procession proceeded down Pennsylvania Avenue to the Capitol where Lincoln was to lie in state in the rotunda. Lincoln's funeral car, draped in black, was pulled by six magnificent white horses. A detachment of black soldiers led the long procession of military and civilian dignitaries. Four thousand black mourners holding hands marched in rows from curb to curb behind the funeral car. Church bells tolled throughout the city. In the distance, cannons rendered the military salute. On both sides of Pennsylvania Avenue a crowd of untold thousands took off their hats and bowed their heads as the funeral car passed.

Lincoln's body lay in state in the Capitol rotunda—again to be viewed by thousands—until Friday morning when it began its long train journey to Springfield, Illinois, where interment would take place. The route would retrace almost exactly that over which Lincoln traveled to Washington from Springfield after being elected president in 1860, a route of seventeen hundred miles, passing through many of the large cities of the East and Midwest.

In each of these cities Lincoln's coffin was taken from the train, and a massive public funeral was held. The coffin was opened at each funeral, and Lincoln's body was again viewed by an estimated one million mourners. Before reaching Springfield, funerals were held in these places: Baltimore; Harrisburg, Pennsylvania; Philadelphia; New York City; Buffalo; Cleveland; Columbus; Indianapolis; Michigan City, Indiana; Chicago.

In his beautiful elegy, "When Lilacs Last in the Dooryard

In Chicago, thirty-six maidens in white surround Lincoln's hearse as it passes through the funeral arch.

At left, a pause in Lincoln's funeral procession on Pennsylvania Avenue.

Bloom'd," Walt Whitman, who had often seen Lincoln in Washington, described the sorrowful journey of the funeral train:

> *Coffin that passes through lanes and streets,*
> *Through day and night with the great cloud*
>   *darkening the land,*
> *With the countless torches lit, with the silent sea of*
>   *faces and the unbared heads,*
> *With the waiting depot, the arriving coffin, and the*
>   *sombre faces,*
> *With the dirges through the night, with the thousand*
>   *voices rising strong and solemn,*
> *With all the mournful voices of the dirges pour'd*
>   *around the coffin,*
> *The dim-lit churches and the shuddering*
>   *organs—where amid these you journey,*
> *With the tolling, tolling bells' perpetual clang,*
> *Here, coffin that slowly passes,*
> *I give you my sprig of lilac.*

At last, on May 3, the train reached Springfield, where the final funeral and ceremonies were held. On the morning of May 4, General Joseph Hooker, one of Lincoln's wartime generals, led a long procession to Oak Ridge cemetery, where Lincoln's coffin was taken to the family vault. The president's large coffin was placed beside a smaller one that was already there. It held the body of the Lincolns' son Willie, who had died in the White House at the age of eleven.

THREE

The Long Quest for a Memorial

Hardly had the last funeral been held than friends and admirers of the martyred president began to call for a memorial in his honor. With remarkable speed, in March 1867, Congress passed a law establishing a Lincoln Monument Association. The association began its work enthusiastically with an invitation to Clarke Mills, the most famous American sculptor of his day, to submit his ideas for a monument to Lincoln. Mills's reputation as a creator of public sculpture rested on a solid body of work. Among his major achievements were the statue of Freedom which crowns the dome of the Capitol in Washington, D.C., and the statue of Andrew Jackson on horseback in Lafayette Square across from the White House.

Sculptor Mills turned quickly to his task and presented to the association his design for a memorial to Lincoln. His plans called for a monument seventy feet high topped by a huge figure of Lincoln. The president would be surrounded by thirty-

Wreaths for Mr. Lincoln on the commemoration of his 182nd birthday, February 12, 1991.

one foot soldiers and standing statesmen and six mounted cavalrymen, all of "colossal size."

The association promptly accepted Clarke Mills's plans, and in doing so demonstrated the intense feelings of resentment that prevailed in the aftermath of the Civil War. The men of the association, all Northerners, wanted to portray Lincoln as a conquering war hero who had crushed the rebellious states of the Confederacy. They were not interested in showing the forgiving, humanitarian side of the great president.

Congress appropriated no money to build the monument to Lincoln. Instead, they authorized every postmaster in the country to collect voluntary donations from citizens and send them to the postmaster general in Washington; the funds would then be turned over to the Lincoln Monument Association. The plan received little publicity, and few contributions came in. During the period of waiting, the enthusiasm of the association seemed to ebb. Their attitude may have been influenced by their daily view of the stump of the Washington Monument sitting unfinished on the Mall. Begun in 1848, work on the monument to George Washington was halted in 1854 and did not resume until 1880. Finally, after thirty-seven years, the Washington Monument was completed in 1885.

Although the Lincoln Monument Association ceased to exist and Mills's design was forgotten, the idea of a memorial to President Lincoln stayed alive. The strongest voice for a memorial became that of Illinois senator Shelby Cullom. He had known Lincoln well and had admired him as a great and humane leader. Indeed, it was said that Senator Cullom looked like Lincoln, talked like him, and had the same genuine fondness for the plain people of the world that Lincoln had displayed.

Over a number of years Senator Cullom introduced bills into the Senate calling for the building of a memorial to Lincoln, but they were all unsuccessful, usually because they were not favorably reported out of committee. Old and in ill health, Cullom knew that his time in the Senate as well as his time on earth was short. In 1910 he sought the help of Congressman Joseph Cannon, Speaker of the House of Representatives and one of the most powerful men that legislative body had ever known. Cannon was also from Illinois, a contemporary and admirer of Lincoln. Together Cannon and Cullom drafted a Lincoln Memorial bill, which Cullom introduced in the Senate and Cannon in the House. This time the bill passed both houses of Congress and was signed into law by President William Howard Taft on February 19, 1911.

According to Smith D. Fry, historian of the Capitol at that time, Senator Cullom, when he heard that the president had signed the bill, said, "Now, Lord, let thy servant depart in peace."

But the senator did not depart before he had time to serve on the Lincoln Memorial Commission that the bill established. And so skillful had he and "Uncle Joe" Cannon been in drafting the bill that this time the commission could hardly fail to succeed. In the first place, the bill designated the president as chairman of the commission. In the second place, it appropriated two million dollars to build the memorial. Two million dollars was by far the largest sum that Congress had ever appropriated for a public monument or memorial and, in 1911, was a very considerable amount of money.

President Taft appointed Senator Cullom, House Speaker Cannon, and four other members of the House and Senate to serve with him on the Lincoln Memorial Commission. The commission held its first meeting on March 4, 1911. With money behind it as well as the power of the presidential office and dedicated members such as Cullom and Cannon, the commission could scarcely fail to achieve its purpose of building a memorial to Abraham Lincoln.

But that would be only one level of success. True success

could only be achieved by selecting the right memorial and the right location. From the outset the commission correctly identified its two essential tasks as answering these questions: What kind of memorial would be best for President Lincoln? Where should it be placed?

Finding the answers to those questions took four years. Many ideas poured into the commission, and most had to be taken seriously. Congressman James McCleary of Minnesota proposed that the memorial take the form of a two-hundred-foot-wide highway between Washington, D.C., and Gettysburg. Along the highway would be placed patriotic statues and other memorials to Lincoln. The budding automobile industry in America strongly supported Congressman McCleary's idea. Some persons advocated a glorious Abraham Lincoln memorial park in the nation's capital; others wanted a monumental triumphal arch at some main entrance into the city. Because of its symbolism of unity, a memorial bridge across the Potomac connecting Arlington National Cemetery with Washington was proposed. Ideas for great pyramids and obelisks like the Washington Monument were submitted. Many ideas for statues were presented to the commission.

From the beginning the commission was committed to the belief that a statue of Lincoln should be a part of the memorial. But a statue alone was not enough; statues of Lincoln had already begun to appear in several American cities, including one in Washington, D.C., paid for by the contributions of private citizens. The commission was determined that the statue should be contained in a structure that would itself be an important part of the memorial.

As vexing as the nature of the memorial, was the question of where it should be placed. The law authorizing the memorial specified that it be located in the nation's capital but left the exact placement to the commission. Railroad officials lobbied to have the memorial near Union Station, but the commission

In 1911 and 1912 many proposals for a Lincoln Memorial, such as these, were submitted to the Lincoln Memorial Commission. Below, a view of the land reclaimed from the Potomac marshes between 1882 and 1902, which ultimately became the site of the Lincoln Memorial.

rejected that location as being too busy and lacking the proper dignity. Some thought the memorial should be near the Capitol; but the space would be crowded, and the commission agreed that the memorial to Lincoln should not have to compete with any other public structure. The grounds of the Soldiers' Home and Fort Stevens, both Washington-area sites, were suggested but not given serious consideration, partly because of their military nature.

As early as 1901 the Park Commission had recommended that if a Lincoln Memorial were built, it should be located in Potomac Park. Between 1882 and 1902 the swampy, marshy tidal basin of the Potomac River had been drained and filled; but when the Lincoln Memorial Commission began looking for a site, the tidal basin was a "park" in name only. Treeless, forlorn, still swampy to some extent, isolated from metropolitan Washington, the tidal basin as a suitable site for a memorial to the Great Emancipator required a great deal of imagination.

Joseph Cannon, the most powerful member of the commission except for President Taft, was bitterly opposed to the Potomac Park site. He called it a "God forsaken," mosquito-infested spot that was good for nothing and vowed he would never let a memorial to Lincoln be built there. "Don't put the memorial here, boys," he said once when the commission was looking at the Potomac Park site. "Why, the malarial ague from these mosquitoes would shake it to pieces."

But some members of the Lincoln Memorial Commission, including President Taft and other influential persons interested in the memorial, had the vision to see the immense possibilities in a Potomac Park site on the banks of the Potomac River. John Hay, one of President Lincoln's personal secretaries and later secretary of state, strongly favored the Potomac Park site. "His monument should stand alone," Hay wrote, "remote from the common habitations of man, apart from the business and turmoil of the city, isolated, distinguished, and serene."

One compelling argument for the Potomac Park site was that it would place the Lincoln Memorial on the axis of the Capitol and the Washington Monument, in keeping with the plan for a grand ceremonial avenue or mall designed for Washington in 1791 by the architect Pierre Charles L'Enfant. Thus the Lincoln Memorial would face the monument to the nation's first president and the Capitol of the Union, which Lincoln gave his life to preserve. From this location the memorial would also be in view of Robert E. Lee's house in Arlington National Cemetery across the Potomac.

The Washington, D.C., Commission of Fine Arts was created by Congress in 1910 and charged with the responsibility of recommending or concurring in the location and design of all public buildings, memorials, and monuments in the city. Its first important act was to recommend the Potomac Park site as the location of the Lincoln Memorial. The Lincoln Memorial Commission accepted the Fine Arts Commission's recommendation on February 3, 1912, and even Representative Joseph Cannon was finally persuaded that this spot on the banks of the Potomac was the best place to build a memorial to Lincoln.

The next task was to find the right architect to design the Lincoln Memorial.

Henry Bacon.

FOUR

A Man for the Memorial:
Henry Bacon

Henry Bacon's life seemed to be an almost uncanny preparation for his crowning architectural achievement: the creation of the Lincoln Memorial. He was born in 1866, the year after Lincoln's death, and grew up in the years when the Civil War, Reconstruction, and Lincoln were still topics of intense daily discussion everywhere in the country. Both of Bacon's parents were from Massachusetts; but Bacon was born in Watseka, Illinois, where his father, a civil engineer, was employed in the early development of the Illinois Central Railroad.

Soon after his birth, Bacon's family moved to Wilmington, North Carolina, where his father became a government engineer in charge of Cape Fear River improvements. Bacon went to school in Wilmington until he was fifteen, at which time his parents sent him to Chauncy Hall School in Boston to finish his secondary education. After graduating from Chauncy Hall School, Bacon enrolled at the University of Illinois, but his stay there was short. He had already made up his mind that he wanted to be an architect; and in the late nineteenth century in America, the way to become one was to work and study in a good architectural firm.

After just one year at Illinois, Bacon left the university and was accepted as apprentice draftsman in the architectural offices of Chamberlain and Whidden in Boston. He did so well there that he was invited to join McKim, Mead, and White, at that time the leading firm of architects in America. One of the partners, Charles Follen McKim, had a strong and deep love of classical Greek and Roman architecture, which he quickly passed on to the new young man in the office, Henry Bacon.

At the age of twenty-three, while still with McKim, Mead, and White, Bacon applied for a Rotch Traveling Scholarship, which paid all the winner's expenses for two years of travel and study in Europe. This scholarship, funded by wealthy Boston architect Arthur Rotch, was open to young architects of unusual promise who had worked at least two years in a Boston office. Although Bacon was now in a New York office, his two years in Boston with an architectural firm made him eligible for the highly prized Rotch scholarship. The strong recommendation of an architect of Charles McKim's stature assured him of winning.

In Europe Bacon spent several months in Italy studying Romanesque and Renaissance architecture, but in Greece he fell under the spell of the Parthenon, the sculpture from the Temple of Zeus, and other marvels of Greek and pre-Hellenic culture. Bacon returned from his European study with a deep love of classical Greek architecture and of the perfect union of architecture and sculpture that would be a guiding force throughout his professional life.

Back in America, Bacon rejoined McKim, Mead, and White as a full-fledged architect, and worked on the design and construction of many important public buildings in New York and other Eastern cities. Soon he took another step in the direction

The Parthenon, often considered the greatest masterpiece of Greek architecture, inspired Henry Bacon's vision of the Lincoln Memorial.

that was leading him to a seemingly inevitable destiny as the creator of a memorial to Abraham Lincoln. In 1892 plans were well in progress for a huge Chicago World's Fair to celebrate the 400th anniversary of Columbus's discovery of America. Plans called for the creation of many monumental buildings in the classical tradition to house exhibitions from all over the world. The firm of McKim, Mead, and White was called in to design some of the buildings, including the colossal and highly decorated Agricultural Building. Bacon was quickly involved in the design work for the World's Fair buildings and was sent to Chicago as executive architect to oversee the execution of the designs.

A MEMORIAL FOR MR. LINCOLN

In charge of the overall planning of the layout of the Chicago World's Fair was Daniel Hudson Burnham, an almost legendary figure in the history of American architecture. The term "skyscraper" is said to have first been used to describe a building in Chicago designed by Burnham (ten stories!), and he later designed the Flatiron Building in New York, that city's first skyscraper. Burnham also became one of the pioneers of city planning in America. In Chicago, Henry Bacon came under Burnham's watchful eyes. The great architect was impressed by the knowledge, inventiveness, and love of monumental architecture that the young man from McKim, Mead, and White displayed.

The Chicago World's Fair was a great success, and the magnificence of the White City, as the Fair's buildings were called, enhanced the reputations of all the architects who created it. In 1897 Bacon left McKim, Mead, and White and practiced under his own name for the rest of his life. Bacon was a highly successful architect, designing many important buildings, principally in the East. Among his major works were the Danforth Memorial Library in Paterson, New Jersey; the train station in Naugatuck, Connecticut; and the Union Square Savings Bank in New York City. Perhaps memories of his civil engineer father inspired his design of the Memorial Bridge in Naugatuck.

From the time of his studies in Greece and Italy, Bacon had been deeply interested in the combination of architecture and sculpture. In pursuit of this interest he began to work with Daniel Chester French, a sculptor of growing reputation who also had worked at the World's Fair. Over time Bacon and French formed a professional relationship and a close friendship, both of which were to last a lifetime. Together they worked on some fifty monuments and memorials such as the monument to Henry Wadsworth Longfellow in Cambridge, Massachusetts, and to James Oglethorpe, founder of

40   *The Lincoln Memorial offers some of the best*
views of Washington.

the Georgia colony, in Savannah, Georgia. Most significant in terms of their future work together was their collaboration in 1911 on an Abraham Lincoln monument for the state capitol grounds in Lincoln, Nebraska.

AMONG HIS MANY public duties after the Chicago World's Fair, Daniel Burnham was chairman of the Washington, D.C., Commission of Fine Arts, and one of the tasks of the commission was to recommend an architect to design the Lincoln Memorial. From the outset Burnham was sure that the right architect for this monumental undertaking was Henry Bacon. From Bacon's work on the Chicago World's Fair buildings, Burnham knew that he had the technical background, the imagination, and the drive for perfection to design a Lincoln Memorial that could take its place in the grand design of the Mall with the Washington Monument and the Capitol. Upon Burnham's recommendation, the Lincoln Memorial Commission invited Bacon to submit a tentative design for a memorial.

Bacon knew that designing the Lincoln Memorial in Washington, D.C., would be the capstone of his career. More than that, it seemed that his whole life had been moving toward this moment of fulfillment: the apprenticeship to McKim, a lover of classical Greek and Roman architecture; the Rotch scholarship, which made study in Greece possible; the work on monumental buildings at the World's Fair; the friendship of the great Daniel Burnham; the years of collaboration with such a fine sculptor as Daniel French.

Bacon immediately began to give intense thought to the memorial and made experimental sketches. He was aware of the report of a committee that had been appointed by the Senate in 1901 to make recommendations for the future erection of public buildings and monuments in Washington. About a possible Lincoln Memorial, the committee had written:

The names of the thirty-six states in the Union at the time of Lincoln's death are inscribed on the frieze above the memorial's colonnade. The dates of statehood appear in Roman numerals.

The attic walls are decorated with festoons in bas-relief, representing the forty-eight states in the Union when the Lincoln Memorial was dedicated in 1922. Both the attic and frieze decorations were carved by Ernest C. Bairstow, an architectural sculptor who lived in Washington, D.C. Bairstow also did the lettering of Lincoln's speeches on the north and south walls of the memorial as well as the inscription above Lincoln's statue. He did the carving and lettering during the final two years of the Memorial's construction.

Whatever may be the exact form selected for the memorial to Lincoln, in type it should possess the quality of universality, and also it should have a character essentially different from that of any monument either existing in the District or hereafter to be erected.

Two of the committee members had been Burnham and McKim, and Bacon understood their artistic minds well. When they talked about "universality" and "a character essentially distinct," he knew exactly what they were talking about.

Bacon knew that the Lincoln Memorial Commission also had set down ideas about the memorial. They wanted to avoid any competition with the Washington Monument and the Capitol. Therefore, they said, the Lincoln Memorial should not have great height, and it should not have a dome. It should, however, have strong horizontal lines. Bacon agreed with all of the commission's thoughts.

Bacon submitted his plans and design in the fall of 1912. Approval came quickly from both the Lincoln Memorial and Fine Arts commissions and from Congress, and on February 1, 1913, the president signed the final approval. That same day the Lincoln Memorial Commission named Henry Bacon to be the architect of the memorial.

Bacon's conception of the memorial was masterful in its blending of grandeur and simplicity. His plans projected a memorial that appealed to the emotions with a statue of the great president in a noble setting. Bacon wrote in his notes, ". . . the most important object is the statue of Lincoln, which is placed in the center of the Memorial, and by virtue of its imposing position in the place of honor, the gentleness, power and intelligence of the man, expressed as far as possible by the sculptor's art, predominates."

But in Bacon's vision, the memorial should appeal not only to the heart but also to the head, the intellect, and to that end he specified that Lincoln's wise and beautifully expressed words, which had given the Union courage and a sense of purpose, should be an integral part of the memorial. The figure of Lincoln would be in a large central chamber; his Gettysburg Address and his Second Inaugural Address would be engraved on the walls of smaller flanking chambers.

The memorial structure Bacon envisioned to contain Lincoln's statue and the great speeches would be a modified Greek temple. Bacon turned the temple so that its side was at right angles to the Mall; this created the desired "strong horizontal lines" and served as a forceful terminus for the western end of the Mall. Bacon brilliantly solved the problem of entering the templelike building from the side rather than from the front, as would have been the case with a classic Greek temple. He designed a great sweep of wide steps leading up to the memorial and replaced anything that might have looked like a formal doorway with a mammoth opening to the central chamber.

In Bacon's design the central block of the memorial containing the statue and the speeches would be enclosed by thirty-six columns forming a surrounding porch and representing the thirty-six states in the Union at the time of Lincoln's death. The names of these states would be cut into the frieze above the colonnade. Another departure from the Greek temple form would be a recessed attic, corresponding in size to that of the chamber block below. The outer walls of the attic would be decorated with the names of the forty-eight states that comprised the United States at the time the Lincoln Memorial was built, together with the dates of their admission to the Union.

Bacon saw in the memorial structure, the statue of Lincoln, and his immortal words a perfect coming together of architecture, art, literature, and history.

❧ FIVE

Building the Memorial

Not everyone was pleased with Henry Bacon's plans for
the Lincoln Memorial. Descriptions of the projected memorial
in newspapers, magazines, and professional journals stirred up
controversy among artists, architects, historians, and just plain
people who had their own feelings about Lincoln. The most
often-heard criticism was that a Greek temple was not appropriate for a man of Lincoln's humble log cabin origins, a plain-
speaking American folk hero, a down-to-earth man of the
people. His statue would look out of place there, they said, un-
comfortable, maybe even ridiculous.

Some art historians complained that such a combination
of grandiose architecture and large sculpture was of a past era,
old-fashioned, out of step with modern art and architectural
thinking. The innovative and influential American architect,
Frank Lloyd Wright, wrote disparagingly of the "falsely tradi-
tional" Olympian character of the memorial.

But Bacon had many supporters, and among the first to

Henry Bacon searched all over northern Virginia for mature American boxwood and holly to transplant around the Memorial before its dedication. The boxwood and holly provide a feeling of warmth and are excellent softening counterpoints to the memorial's formality.

speak in defense of the modified Greek temple form was his friend, Daniel Chester French. "Many people say they are unable to associate Lincoln with a Greek temple, as they believe the memorial to be," French wrote, "but to me nothing else would have been suitable, for the Greeks alone were able to express in their buildings, monuments and statues the highest attributes and the greatest beauty known to man. The memorial tells you just what manner of man you are come to pay homage to; his simplicity, his grandeur and his power."

Aware of the controversy but believing in his own vision, Bacon began to prepare the detailed drawings necessary for constructing the memorial. That work and contracting with an engineering firm and construction companies took a full year.

On February 12, 1914, the 105th anniversary of Lincoln's birth, Bacon and a small group of Washington officials stood in the bitter cold near the banks of the frozen Potomac River and bowed their heads in a quiet ground-breaking ceremony. Senator Shelby Cullom, who more than anyone else was the father of the Lincoln Memorial, was not in the group. He had died on January 28, just two weeks before the ground-breaking. But before he died, the determined senator from Illinois had the satisfaction of knowing that the task of creating the memorial to Abraham Lincoln was in Henry Bacon's capable hands and that it would be built.

Work on the memorial began immediately after the ground-breaking, and for the next eight years—in fact, for the rest of his life—the Lincoln Memorial became Bacon's absorbing interest.

By curious coincidence, the man chosen to be the chief engineer for building the memorial was L. J. Lincoln, a distant relative of the Great Emancipator. Separate Washington companies won contracts for digging and building the memorial's sub-foundation and upper foundation and for building the super-structure. Such a massive structure to be built on drained and

filled land required the most stable of sub-foundations. To assure that stability, 122 solid poured-concrete piers with steel reinforcing rods were driven to bedrock at depths of from 44 to 65 feet.

The upper foundation is made up of a series of concrete piers set on top of the sub-foundation piers; the upper piers are about 45 feet high; they are joined together by poured concrete arches, which form the floor of the memorial.

The height of the memorial's great superstructure is 79 feet 10 inches from the top of the foundation to the top of the attic. The Doric colonnade around the building is 188 feet in length and 118 feet 6 inches in width. The columns in the colonnade are 44 feet from the bottom joint to the top of the cap, and each column is composed of eleven drums, excluding the cap. The interior Ionic columns that divide the three chambers are 50 feet from the floor to the top of the cap. The central chamber containing Lincoln's statue is 60 feet wide, 74 feet deep. The two side chambers containing Lincoln's speeches are 63 feet wide, 38 feet deep.

The memorial is built of a variety of materials including marble, granite, limestone, brick, and concrete. The foundations and floor slabs are constructed of concrete, most of which is reinforced. The exterior of the building is built of white Colorado marble, which came from quarries located near the town of Marble, about three hundred miles west of Denver. Colorado marble was selected because of its superior qualities of color, texture, and uniformity and because no other quarries were known to produce high quality stones of the size required. Some of the Colorado marble stones weigh over 23 tons each.

The interior walls and columns are made of Indiana limestone. The interior floor, which is two inches thick, and the wall base are of pink Tennessee marble. The ceiling, 60 feet above the floor, is made up of bronze beams and panels of Alabama marble about one inch thick.

The Lincoln Memorial in an early stage of construction.

French and Bacon quickly discovered that natural lighting was insufficient and too variable to satisfactorily illuminate Lincoln's statue and some parts of the memorial building. The ceiling panels of white Alabama marble were soaked in paraffin so that they would more effectively transmit light from the skylight and from a carefully planned lighting system installed above the ceiling by the General Electric Company.

Observant visitors to the memorial will note that there is a slight inward tilt to the columns. The ancient Greek architects of the Parthenon and other beautiful temples discovered that rows of perfectly straight columns give the effect that the building is bulging at the top. They corrected this optical illusion with the inward tilt of the columns, a technique employed by Bacon in the Lincoln Memorial.

Work on the memorial went forward steadily from 1914 until the United States entered World War I in 1917. Construction slowed then because of the manpower shortage, but it never stopped completely. At the conclusion of the war in 1918, work resumed its normal pace until the memorial was completed in 1922.

From the beginning, every detail of construction was carried out under Henry Bacon's watchful eyes. Most of the fee of $150,000 he received for his work on the memorial went into drawings, models, and trips almost every week for eight years from his home in New York to Washington. He once said that of all the work he had ever undertaken, the Lincoln Memorial was "the most unprofitable financially." He never had any doubt, however, that from an artistic and professional point of view, the memorial was the most profitable, the crowning achievement of a rich life in architecture.

CONSTRUCTION of the memorial building was well underway before a sculptor was chosen to create the statue of Lincoln that would occupy the central chamber. Selection of the sculptor was in the hands of the Lincoln Memorial Commission, but it was understood that Bacon would have a say in the choice. Bacon had never had the slightest doubt about who the sculptor should be: his old friend and colleague Daniel French. Not only was French generally regarded at that time as America's most

FOUR SCORE AND SEVEN YEARS
AGO OUR FATHERS BROUGHT FORTH
ON THIS CONTINENT A NEW NATION
CONCEIVED IN LIBERTY AND DEDICA-
TED TO THE PROPOSITION THAT ALL
MEN ARE CREATED EQUAL ·
NOW WE ARE ENGAGED IN A GREAT
CIVIL WAR TESTING WHETHER THAT
NATION OR ANY NATION SO CON-
CEIVED AND SO DEDICATED CAN LONG
ENDURE · WE ARE MET ON A GREAT
BATTLEFIELD OF THAT WAR · WE HAVE
COME TO DEDICATE A PORTION OF
THAT FIELD AS A FINAL RESTING
PLACE FOR THOSE WHO HERE GAVE
THEIR LIVES THAT THAT NATION
MIGHT LIVE · IT IS ALTOGETHER FIT-
TING AND PROPER THAT WE SHOULD
DO THIS · BUT IN A LARGER SENSE
WE CAN NOT DEDICATE—WE CAN NOT
CONSECRATE—WE CAN NOT HALLOW—
THIS GROUND · THE BRAVE MEN LIV-
ING AND DEAD WHO STRUGGLED HERE
HAVE CONSECRATED IT FAR ABOVE
OUR POOR POWER TO ADD OR DETRACT.
THE WORLD WILL LITTLE NOTE NOR
LONG REMEMBER WHAT WE SAY HERE
BUT IT CAN NEVER FORGET WHAT THEY
DID HERE · IT IS FOR US THE LIVING
RATHER TO BE DEDICATED HERE TO
THE UNFINISHED WORK WHICH THEY
WHO FOUGHT HERE HAVE THUS FAR
SO NOBLY ADVANCED · IT IS RATHER FOR
US TO BE HERE DEDICATED TO THE
GREAT TASK REMAINING BEFORE US—
THAT FROM THESE HONORED DEAD
WE TAKE INCREASED DEVOTION TO
THAT CAUSE FOR WHICH THEY GAVE THE
LAST FULL MEASURE OF DEVOTION—
THAT WE HERE HIGHLY RESOLVE THAT
THESE DEAD SHALL NOT HAVE DIED IN
VAIN—THAT THIS NATION UNDER GOD
SHALL HAVE A NEW BIRTH OF FREEDOM—
AND THAT GOVERNMENT OF THE PEOPLE
BY THE PEOPLE FOR THE PEOPLE SHALL
NOT PERISH FROM THE EARTH ·

The Gettysburg Address is carved on the south wall of the Memorial.

prominent public sculptor, but he and Bacon had already worked together on the successful Lincoln monument in Lincoln, Nebraska.

As the year 1914 came to a close, the commission made its official announcement. Daniel Chester French would sculpt the statue for the Lincoln Memorial.

Daniel Chester French in his studio at Chesterwood, his home in Stockbridge, Massachusetts.

✒ SIX

Creating Lincoln's Statue:
Daniel Chester French

Daniel Chester French was seventeen years older than Henry Bacon and did not begin the great work of his life, the heroic statue of Abraham Lincoln for the Lincoln Memorial, until he was sixty-four years old. Born in 1850, the youngest of four children in a well-to-do New England family, he was fifteen by the time the Civil War ended, old enough to have known men going into and returning from battle, old enough to have read the words of the Gettysburg Address and the Second Inaugural Address in the Boston newspapers.

French's father was a lawyer who commuted to his office in Boston by train so that he and his family could enjoy rural life on a small farm near Concord. After secondary school, French had no desire to go to college; he did some work on the family farm and, with plentiful spare time, began to make clay figures of animals: cats, dogs, and wild creatures.

One figure that he called "The Wounded Deer" was a mirror of young French's sensitive nature. Hunting at Walden Pond a few years earlier, he had shot a deer. His first feeling was one of elation at his good shot, but when he found the deer, he saw that it was not dead. The wounded animal raised its head and gazed at the boy with what he thought was a look of reproach in its eyes. Then it shuddered, put its head on his leg, and died. French was overwhelmed with pity and remorse. He never forgot that moment and he never hunted deer again. In the clay statuette, he tried to express something of what he had felt that day.

May Alcott, a neighbor of the Frenches and sister of the famous author of *Little Women*, heard about Daniel French's clay figures and came to look at them. She was astonished at his natural talent and his ability to express his feelings in clay. Herself an artist and art teacher who had studied in Paris for several years, May Alcott gave French drawing lessons and taught him how to make an armature, a frame for supporting clay or plaster in large figures. Then she gave him some wooden sculptor's tools and told him to keep working.

French did keep working and never seemed to tire of making figures in clay. He went to New York to study sculpture and drawing but returned to the family farm after only a few months, dissatisfied with city living. Rather than being a setback to his artistic ambitions, French's homecoming turned out to be a move that launched his career. The town of Concord, where the first battle of the Revolutionary War had been fought, wanted to erect a statue of a Minuteman for the centennial celebration in 1886, less than two years away. The Concord statue committee asked French if he would like to submit a model for the statue.

He would! French went to work feverishly on drawings, and in a month presented a small clay model to the committee. They liked what they saw and gave French his first commission as a professional sculptor. There were, however, some conditions. The town would pay all of his expenses in making the

Although many visitors to the Lincoln Memorial give only a passing glance to the murals mounted high on the north and south walls, they are an integral part of the memorial as conceived by Henry Bacon. Each mural is sixty feet long and twelve feet high; the canvas on which each is painted weighs six hundred pounds. The main theme of the mural above the Gettysburg Address on the south wall is freedom. The central panel shows the Angel of Truth giving freedom to the slave and symbolizes Lincoln's emancipation of the American slaves. In the central panel of the mural above the Second Inaugural Address on the north wall, the Angel of Truth joins the hands of figures representing the North and South, symbolizing Lincoln's triumph in preserving the Union. The Lincoln Memorial murals were painted by Jules Guérin, an artist noted for his murals in many public buildings in U.S. cities. Guérin was born in St. Louis, Missouri, in 1866, just one year after the end of the Civil War.

statue, but there was not enough money to pay him a fee. He would have to contribute his services. French did not hesitate. Here at last was his chance to be a true sculptor, and money did not matter. He accepted the Concord statue committee's offer.

Immediately French was beset by doubts, not about agreeing to work for no money but by doubts more fundamental than that. Could he do it? Could he make a real statue? He had sculpted many small animals and the heads of a few friends, but could he make a seven-foot statue of a Colonial Minuteman who had lived a hundred years ago?

"I don't know if I can do it," French confided to a friend, "but a year from now I'll know."

French worked for months, often ten hours a day, beginning with a three-foot model on which he labored to get just the right pose. In this cradle of the American Revolutionary War, French discovered that his neighbors could find in their attics everything he needed to guide his work: authentic Minuteman clothes, a Colonial period musket and powder horn, even a hundred-year-old plow—for as French conceived his statue, the Minuteman was a farmer who carried a gun to defend his country.

When French finished his statue in clay, it was cast in plaster and then bronze by professional casters in Boston. From the moment of its unveiling, the Minuteman was a great success, and from the day of its dedication has guarded North Bridge, Concord, with an air of sturdy defiance, just as the bridge was guarded in 1776 by colonists who were ready to drop their plows and fight British troops at a minute's notice.

French studied for a while in Italy after completing the Minuteman but remained essentially a self-taught artist. Although the Minuteman of Concord brought him a measure of recognition, his progress in a career as a sculptor was leisurely. By the time he was forty, he had executed only seven statues for display in public parks and buildings, but they included some outstanding work: a bust of Ralph Waldo Emerson; a large seated bronze statue of John Harvard, first benefactor of Harvard University; a statuary group called "War and Peace" for the United States customs house in St. Louis; a statue of the ancient Greek historian Herodotus for the Library of Congress.

Although his body of work was small, its quality was such that French was asked to take part in preparations for the World's Fair in Chicago in 1893. The opportunities for sculpture at the great exhibition opened the gates of a creative energy reservoir that would flow unchecked through the rest of French's life. Arriving at the vast Chicago fairgrounds early in 1892, he began work immediately on a twelve-foot model for what would become a sixty-four-foot-high statue of a woman to represent the Republic. He then worked with another fine sculptor, Edward C. Potter, to create five sculpture groups including a masterpiece called "The Triumph of Columbus." This astonishing sculptural output was completed in a year and a half and was ready for the opening of the great world exhibition in 1893.

Millions of Americans saw Daniel French's work at the Chicago World's Fair, and after that he was in constant demand as a public sculptor. During the remainder of his life, French created 120 statues and other sculptures for parks and buildings all over the United States and one important work in Paris; on fifty of these projects he collaborated with Henry Bacon.

The selection of Daniel French to sculpt the statue of Abraham Lincoln for the Lincoln Memorial brought him together once more with Bacon for what would be their last and greatest collaboration. From the very beginning of their work on the memorial their goal was to bring about a perfect unity of statue and building.

Although French was at the height of his abilities and had

French's seven-foot model of the Lincoln statue was prepared between April and October 1916.

been creating much-admired public sculptures for forty years, he admitted to his daughter Margaret that being chosen to sculpt the statue of Lincoln for the great memorial in Washington made him feel very humble and "a little panicky." There were already many fine sculptures of Lincoln. French wondered if he had anything fresh to contribute. But, his daughter said, her father always had feelings of uncertainty until he actually "got his fingers into the clay."

French went immediately to Washington to see the still-unfinished memorial building and to have long conversations with Bacon. French was awed by the great templelike structure of gleaming white marble that his friend had designed. And to think that it was being built to contain but a single statue! Probably the feeling of panic returned as French stood for the first time in the central chamber of the memorial and tried to imagine what his figure of Lincoln would look like.

In their first talks Bacon and French made two important decisions. The first was that the figure of Lincoln had to be seated. A standing figure among the memorial's many Doric and Ionic columns would create too much vertical thrust. Also, a standing figure of adequate size would put Lincoln's head too far above the eye of a person inside the memorial. The second decision was that Lincoln should not be seated in an armchair such as he might have used during his lifetime. Such a chair would be too informal, too "folksy." They decided on a curule chair, the type of massive, formal chair from Roman antiquity in which only the highest civil officers were privileged to sit. The curule chair would provide the proper dignity for Lincoln without giving any appearance that he was sitting on a throne.

In their initial discussions Bacon and French did not make a decision about what kind of material would be used in making the statue. Neither did they try to determine the statue's size. The contract French signed with the Lincoln Memorial Commission simply stated that the statue would not be less than ten feet in height and that it would be cast in statuary bronze or cut from marble.

French returned to his home and studio in a lovely rural area near Stockbridge, Massachusetts, and began to work. His first step was to review the great amount of material he had collected when preparing to do the Nebraska Lincoln statue. At that time he had had several talks with Robert Lincoln, the president's only living son; now he dug out his notes on those talks and read them again. He reread biographies of Lincoln. He studied the copy of Lincoln's life mask and plaster casts of Lincoln's hands that he already owned.

French studied photographs of Lincoln that had been taken by Matthew Brady and other photographers during Lincoln's lifetime. He pored over photographs of the many statues of Lincoln that already existed, some by prominent sculptors. They projected Lincoln in almost every possible pose: the railsplitter, the orator, the young lawyer, the emancipator; they showed him praying, dying, surrounded by his generals, seated on a throne, riding horseback.

Some of these statues were well done, some poorly done, but they all made a statement about some phase of Lincoln's life. French wanted his statue of Lincoln to be Lincoln the president, the humanitarian, the preserver of the Union. He wanted the burdens of the Civil War to be reflected in the president's rugged features.

With the decisions about a seated Lincoln and the type of chair already made, French now "got his fingers into the clay" with a small-scale model in which his first concern was form—the shape and composition of the sculpture. He liked the result, and so did Henry Bacon when he came to French's studio to look at it. French then presented the model to the Lincoln Memorial and Fine Arts commissions in Washington and received their immediate approval.

French next made a three-foot model in which he paid

French added the drapery to Lincoln's chair to soften its hard lines.

special attention to Lincoln's hands and head and the position of his feet. French had always felt that hands are especially expressive of personality. He symbolized Lincoln's strength and determination with a clenched left hand and the calm nature of the great president with a relaxed right hand. In the three-foot model French gave a slight inclination to Lincoln's head as if he were listening. French strove to show the power he sensed in the bony ruggedness of Lincoln's face and to add a look of thoughtful concern to the careworn features.

At the end of October 1916, French completed work on a seven-foot enlargement of the three-foot model. In the new model he paid close attention to anatomical accuracy—the physical structure of Lincoln's body—and to further work on the facial expression. With the same care he had given the Minuteman forty years earlier, French made certain that Lincoln's clothes were exactly of the type he would have worn in the 1860s.

The time had come to determine the correct size for the finished statue and the kind of material from which it would be made. French went to Washington and set up a ten-foot plaster model of his statue inside the memorial. Both French and Bacon were shocked at the result. Sitting in the memorial building with its soaring columns and high walls of marble and limestone, the ten-foot Lincoln looked like a pygmy. French and Bacon experimented with photographic enlargements of the statue glued to fiberboard. The enlargements ranged from fourteen to twenty feet. They finally concluded that the finished statue should be nineteen feet high measuring from Lincoln's foot to the top of his head, and that the chair should be twelve-and-a-half feet high. The statue would sit on a pedestal eleven feet high.

During their long sessions in the memorial French and Bacon decided that the statue should not be made of bronze. The dark metal did not seem to be right for the gleaming mar-

The statue of Lincoln being assembled.

IN THIS TEMPLE
AS IN THE HEARTS OF THE PEOPLE
FOR WHOM HE SAVED THE UNION
THE MEMORY OF ABRAHAM LINCOLN
IS ENSHRINED FOREVER

Daniel French and Henry Bacon (right) pose in front of Lincoln's statue as assembling is completed.

ble of the memorial building. They agreed that Lincoln's statue should be carved from white Georgia marble.

It was at about this period that French remarked to an acquaintance, "I have lived with Lincoln so long that I feel as if he were a personal friend."

And now the time had come to bring others into the work. French went to New York early in 1918 to engage the services of the Piccirilli brothers, an Italian-American family whose marble-cutting skills had made them famous among American sculptors. The six Piccirilli brothers worked under the direction of their patriarch father, and they were so accomplished in shaping stone that they could work in relays, one following the other on the same piece of stone, with perfect results. Their workshop covered almost an entire city block, and so great was their backlog of carving assignments that they could not begin to work for French until November 1918.

The statue of Lincoln was so huge that there was no possibility of quarrying one block of marble from which to cut it. Even if such a gigantic piece of stone without imperfections could have been found, it could not have been transported from Georgia to New York. The eventual weight of the statue itself, after all the cutting, was 175 tons.

The art of the marble cutter now took over. Using techniques as ancient as Michelangelo, the Piccirilli brothers worked simultaneously on twenty-eight blocks of marble, "pointing up" French's seven-foot model of the Lincoln statue with an enlarging machine. The Piccirillis completed their carving on November 19, 1919, almost exactly one year from the time they began their work. During much of that year, French had been in the Piccirilli workshop adding his personal touch with hammer and chisel.

The blocks of the statue were shipped immediately to Washington, and their assembling, like the pieces of a giant jigsaw puzzle, began in December. So perfect had the Piccirillis' work been that only the highly trained eye of an expert could detect the slightest seam. When the statue was in place in the memorial, French again took his sculptor's tools and added the final refinements to his greatest masterpiece.

Writing about the Lincoln statue in May 1920, French said, "It is now as technically perfect as I can make it."

And of course it was more than technically perfect. Daniel French's Lincoln was also as artistically perfect as a great sculptor's genius and years of hard work could make it.

❧ SEVEN

Dedication

Memorial Day on May 30, 1922, broke bright and beautiful over Washington, D.C., one of those rare spring days when the nation's capital can match weather with any spot on earth. And on this day, the day America sets aside each year to honor its war dead, a memorial would be dedicated to a man who strove with all his heart and mind for peace but who instead brought his country safely through a tragic war of self-destruction.

By late morning thousands of people were moving toward Potomac Park and settling themselves around the Lincoln Memorial, which seemed to glow as the early sun warmed its white marble columns. The dedication was scheduled to begin at 2:30; well before that time the invited guests—3,500 government officials, diplomats, and private-sector executives—began to arrive. For many invited guests there was standing room only.

The official party headed by President Warren G. Harding

Arrival of President Warren G. Harding and party for the dedication of the Lincoln Memorial.

arrived on schedule. President Harding was accompanied by former President and now Chief Justice William Howard Taft, who was still chairman of the Lincoln Memorial Commission. A special honored guest was Robert Todd Lincoln, son of Abraham Lincoln. Now in retirement, Mr. Lincoln had been a successful corporate lawyer and had served the government as secretary of war and minister to Great Britain. Henry Bacon, Daniel Chester French, and others who had helped to create the Lincoln Memorial were in the official party.

By the time the ceremonies began at 2:45, the crowd around the memorial had grown to fifty thousand. Loudspeakers had been installed so that they could hear the program. A nationwide broadcast of the dedication ceremonies had been arranged, a remarkable feat for a radio industry only two years old.

What radio could not show was the thin line of blue-clad Union veterans and gray-clad Confederate veterans sitting in a front-row place of honor. Most had been boys in their teens when they had carried guns in a war to decide the fate of the nation. Now they were old men in their seventies, citizens of a secure union of forty-eight states, and their presence symbolized Lincoln's counsel to both North and South in his Second Inaugural Address to "bind up the nation's wounds."

As chairman of the Lincoln Memorial Commission, Chief Justice Taft spoke first. "The American people have waited fifty-seven years for a national memorial to Abraham Lincoln," he began. "Those years have faded the figures of his contemporaries, and he stands grandly alone."

As expected, Taft's words etched the greatness of Lincoln. "Justice, truth, patience, mercy and love of his kind; simplicity, courage, sacrifice, and confidence in God were his moral qualities. Clarity of thought and intellectual honesty, self-analysis and strong inexorable logic, supreme common sense, a sympathetic but unerring knowledge of human nature, imagination and limpid purity of style, with a poetic rhythm of the Psalms—these were his intellectual and cultural traits."

Taft spoke of Lincoln's humility and devotion, his "patience under grievous disappointment," his "agony of spirit in the burden he had to carry," his "endurance in a great cause of small obstructive minds." Lincoln's family sorrows, Taft said, and his final tragic death at the moment of victory "form the story of a passion and give him a personality that is as vivid in the hearts of people as if it were but yesterday."

In conclusion, Taft called the memorial itself an altar upon which the ultimate sacrifice was made in the cause of Liberty. "Mr. President," he said, "in the name of the Commission, I have the honor to deliver this Lincoln Memorial into your keeping."

President Harding began his dedication address by accepting the memorial on behalf of the government, and then he said that he wished to speak that day as a grateful American rather than as a public official. Harding was not known as an orator or public speaker; in his presidency, cut short at twenty months by his sudden death in August 1923, he had little opportunity for memorable speeches. But on that Memorial Day in 1922, Harding spoke wisely and with clear insight into the true meaning and importance of the Lincoln Memorial.

"He rose to colossal stature in a day of imperiled union," Harding said in his tribute to Lincoln. "He first appealed, and then commanded, and left the Union secure and the nation supreme."

And then Harding made his essential point. "Lincoln was no superman. Like the great Washington, whose monumental shaft towers nearby as a fit companion to the memorial we dedicate today . . . Lincoln was a very natural human being, with the frailties mixed with the virtues of humanity. There are neither supermen nor demi-gods in the government of kingdoms, empires, or republics. It will be better for our conception of

Robert Todd Lincoln, son of Abraham Lincoln, was an honored guest at the dedication of the Lincoln Memorial.

The crowd gathers for the dedication of the Memorial, May 30, 1922.

government and its institutions if we will understand this fact. It is vastly greater than finding the superman if we justify the confidence that our institutions are capable of bringing into authority, in time of stress, men big enough and strong enough to meet all demands."

With remarkable insight, President Harding concluded, "This memorial, matchless tribute that it is, is less for Abraham Lincoln than for those of us today, and for those who follow after."

President Harding's message was clear: The Lincoln Memorial will always remind us that "government of the people, by the people and for the people" can produce the men and women capable of leading the nation through any crisis.

Following the president's speech, another man spoke, giving the main address of the day, but he had not sat on the speakers' platform because he was black. Instead, the chief usher had escorted him to a segregated, all-Negro section across the road from the rest of the audience, where he sat until he was called upon to speak. He was Dr. Robert R. Moton, principal of Tuskegee Institute.

Dr. Moton was born in 1867, just two years after the Civil War ended. His mother and father worked as slaves on Virginia plantations until the war ended and then continued their work there as free persons. A daughter of the man they worked for taught young Moton to read. Later he worked his way through Hampton Institute in Virginia; he also received a license to practice law by reading law in the office of the superintendent of schools in Farmville, Virginia. Dr. Moton became principal of Tuskegee Institute in Alabama in 1915. During a distinguished career he received honorary degrees from many educational institutions, including Harvard and Howard universities.

In his speech that afternoon of the dedication of the Lincoln Memorial, Dr. Moton reviewed the remarkable progress the American Negro had made in little more than half a cen-

Dr. Robert R. Moton, principal speaker at the Lincoln Memorial dedication ceremonies. In an ugly reminder of the times, Dr. Moton was seated in a segregated part of the audience.

tury of freedom. He spoke of the discrimination that had hindered more progress and urged blacks and whites to join together to complete the work that Abraham Lincoln had begun.

Abraham Lincoln died to save the Union, Dr. Moton said, but in signing the Emancipation Proclamation, "He freed a nation as well as a race."

A view of the north side of the Lincoln Memorial.

❧ EIGHT

A New Symbol for the Nation

ALMOST FROM the day of its dedication all criticism of the Greek temple form of the Lincoln Memorial ended. For millions of Americans the proof was in the viewing. The beauty of the great white marble structure was breathtaking, and the thoughtful figure of Lincoln looked very much at home there. The majestic setting and the dignity yet warmth of the quietly contemplative Lincoln seemed both appropriate to and symbolic of his greatness. Furthermore, the memorial seemed to be an expression of American idealism and of a hope that the nation's leaders would always find within themselves some of Lincoln's qualities.

The memorial quickly took its place in America's everyday culture. Since 1923 its image has been printed on the back of every five-dollar bill issued by the government and from 1959 stamped on the back of every penny. The motion picture industry soon discovered its symbolic value, and most movies

An audience of 75,000 listens as contralto Marian Anderson sings at the Lincoln Memorial, Easter Sunday 1939.

with a Washington background contained at least one view of the new memorial to Lincoln.

The most effective motion picture use of the memorial was in the 1939 film classic, *Mr. Smith Goes to Washington*, starring James Stewart. Stewart plays the role of Jefferson Smith, a naive young idealist from Montana appointed to finish the term of a U.S. senator who has died. The moment Smith gets off the train, he visits Washington's great historic sites and is most awed by the Lincoln Memorial. Later, he describes the experience to his Senate office assistant Saunders (Jean Arthur): "That Lincoln Memorial—gee whiz! Mr. Lincoln, there he is, looking right straight at you as you come up the steps. Just sitting there, like he was waiting for somebody to come along."

Later, disgusted with the corruption he finds in the Senate, Jefferson Smith packs his bags with the intention of going back to Montana. But he cannot resist going to the Lincoln Memorial one more time; and Saunders finds him there, as she is sure she will. With these words she convinces him to stay and fight for what is right: "Mr. Lincoln . . . *was* waiting for somebody. He was waiting for *you*, Jeff." Smith hears the message, looks once more at Lincoln, and returns to the Senate and victory.

But it is in real life that the symbolic force of the Lincoln Memorial has been most dramatically felt. In 1939 the black American singer, Marian Anderson, was scheduled to give a concert in Washington, D.C. The concert sponsor, Howard University, wanted her performance to be in Constitution Hall, at that time Washington's biggest and best concert facility. Miss Anderson was one of the great contraltos of her time or of any time. Arturo Toscanini, the most respected conductor of his day, called her voice one that was heard only once in a hundred years. Isaac Stern, the famed violinist, has known Miss Anderson for many years and describes her voice as "this unbelievable sound that has not been repeated since."

Despite her talent and the fact that she had sung in the

On October 11, 1954, Marian Anderson sang again at the Lincoln Memorial on the occasion of a memorial service for Harold L. Ickes, who died in 1952. As Secretary of the Interior, Ickes approved Ms. Anderson's Lincoln Memorial concert in 1939.

great concert halls of Europe for years, the owners of Constitution Hall, the Daughters of the American Revolution (DAR), refused to let her sing in their building. The DAR policy, they said, was that Constitution Hall was available to white artists only. The United States was still very much a racially segregated nation in 1939, but so renowned was Marian Anderson as a singer that an outcry against the DAR bigotry was heard all over the country. Eleanor Roosevelt, the wife of President Franklin D. Roosevelt, resigned in protest from the DAR when the organization would not change its position on Miss Anderson's concert.

In a solution that made history, Secretary of the Interior Harold L. Ickes agreed to let Marian Anderson's concert be held at the Lincoln Memorial. When Miss Anderson walked onto the steps of the memorial at five o'clock in the afternoon on April 9, an audience of seventy-five thousand crowded around the memorial steps and stretched out on both sides of the reflecting pool for its full length. The audience was mostly black; but thousands of whites were there to hear Miss Anderson sing, and millions of all races heard her on nationwide radio.

The great contralto paused and turned to look at the statue of Abraham Lincoln behind her. Then she took her place behind a battery of microphones, closed her eyes, and in a voice choked with emotion began to sing. Her opening number was "America," and the first words, "My country 'tis of thee, sweet land of liberty . . ." brought a complete hush over the vast audience.

Todd Duncan, himself a talented singer, was one of the people at the Lincoln Memorial that April evening. "My feelings were so deep that I have never forgotten it, and until I leave this earth, I don't think I will ever forget it," he said in a Public Broadcasting System documentary about Marian Anderson. "I have never been so proud to be an American. I have never been so proud to be an American Negro."

The crowd in front of the Lincoln Memorial grew to 250,000 as the participants in the March on Washington in 1963 waited to hear the address of Dr. Martin Luther King, Jr.

Dr. Martin Luther King, Jr. being interviewed inside the Lincoln Memorial on the occasion of the 1963 "March on Washington." Dr. King's "I Have a Dream" speech was the highlight of the rally.

Miss Anderson sang "My Soul Is Anchored in the Lord" and other songs from her rich repertoire to complete the program. After more than fifty years, the recording of her Lincoln Memorial concert remains one of the most frequently requested records from the Library of Congress. Another thirteen years passed before the Daughters of the American Revolution dropped their "white artists only" restriction on Constitution Hall, but Marian Anderson's dramatic performance in the symbolic setting of the Lincoln Memorial helped to focus national attention on the ugly reality of racial inequality in America as it had seldom been focused before.

Twenty-four years later, on August 28, 1963, 250,000 persons gathered in Washington, D.C., for a great civil rights demonstration. Officially named the "March on Washington for Jobs and Freedom," it was led by Dr. Martin Luther King, Jr., and both blacks and whites came from every state in the nation to take part.

More than six hundred buses carried participants from New York City alone. The main purpose of the demonstration was to encourage Congress to pass a bill that would give blacks equal rights with whites. Some important civil rights gains had been made in the years since Marian Anderson had sung at the Lincoln Memorial, but there was still a huge mountain to climb against racial discrimination.

The vast throng assembled at the Washington Monument and, as one newspaper reported, paraded with "discipline, dignity and determination. They were calm and serious." The marchers moved to the Lincoln Memorial and, as in 1939, gathered in front and spread out down both sides of the reflecting pool as far as the eye could see. On this day the number was three times greater than the huge audience that had gathered for Marian Anderson.

The day was hot and humid, as most August days are in Washington. Speaker after speaker took his or her turn behind the microphones, and as the afternoon wore on, the great crowd grew tired, restless, and inattentive. But at about three o'clock the glorious gospel singer Mahalia Jackson stepped forward and sang the spiritual "I've Been 'Buked and I've Been Scorned." Immediately, a quarter of a million listeners fell silent, their attention again focused on the Lincoln Memorial.

And then Martin Luther King, Jr., spoke to the civil rights marchers and to untold millions of radio and television listeners. Standing only a few feet from the statue of the Great Emancipator, Dr. King called the Lincoln Memorial "this hallowed spot," and he spoke against "the manacles of segregation and the chains of discrimination."

But mainly he spoke of his dream that the nation would listen to and begin to live by the words of the Declaration of Independence that "We hold these truths to be self-evident, that all men are created equal." He spoke of his dream of an America where people "will not be judged by the color of their skin, but by the content of their character." He spoke of his dream of a day when the black and white people of this country "will be able to work together, to pray together, to struggle together." If America was to become a truly great nation, he said, these things must happen. Dr. King's moving plea at the Lincoln Memorial for equal rights and dignity for all citizens has become known as his "I Have a Dream" speech.

The next year Congress passed the Civil Rights Act of 1964, prohibiting racial discrimination in public places and encouraging equal educational and employment opportunities. Dr. King was struck down by an assassin's bullet on April 4, 1968, but he had lived to see a beginning made on his dream.

TODAY ANOTHER memorial stands beside the Lincoln Memorial. Since 1982, as Lincoln looks out across the Mall to the Washington Monument and the Capitol in the distance, his gaze

90

Civil rights demonstrators around the reflecting pool in front of the Lincoln Memorial, August 28, 1963.

falls first on the Vietnam Veterans Memorial only six hundred feet away. In some ways it is hard to imagine two memorials so completely different. The Lincoln Memorial is made of gleaming white marble and soars toward the sky. The Vietnam Veterans Memorial is made of black granite and seems to rise from the earth and recede back into it. The Lincoln Memorial is a massive templelike structure with great Greek columns. The Vietnam Veterans Memorial consists of two simple shining walls on which are engraved over fifty-eight thousand names.

On another level the two memorials are alike in some very fundamental ways. Each has its own great emotional power. Both were born out of terrible wars that divided our nation. Both have helped to heal the nation's wounds caused by those wars.

The closeness of the two memorials means that almost everyone who visits one goes to the other. The final words of Lincoln's Second Inaugural Address, engraved on the north wall of his memorial, carry a powerful message for the person who has just come from or who is about to go to the Vietnam Veterans Memorial:

> With malice toward none, with charity for all,
> with firmness in the right as God gives us to see the
>   right,
> let us finish the work we are in,
> to bind up the nation's wounds,
> to care for him who shall have borne the battle,
> and for his widow and his orphans,
> to do all which may achieve and cherish a just and a
> lasting peace among ourselves and with all nations.

The closeness of the Lincoln Memorial
and the Vietnam Veterans Memorial
has a special meaning for Americans today.

The reflecting pool, designed by Henry Bacon, Charles McKim, and others, was not completed at the time the Lincoln Memorial was dedicated. This is an aerial view of the reflecting pool shortly after it was finished in 1923. The reflecting pool is 2000 feet long, 160 feet wide, a shallow basin with a subsidiary pool at its eastern end near the Washington Monument. This early view shows temporary government buildings, which cluttered the Mall during and after World War I but which fortunately have since been removed.

❧ NINE

A Memorial for Mr. Lincoln

THE POWER of the Lincoln Memorial grew on Joseph Cannon, the man—next to Senator Shelby Cullom—most responsible for the law that made the memorial possible. At first he had bitterly opposed placement of the memorial in Potomac Park, but in time he began to see the majesty of the setting. When Cannon retired from the House of Representatives after fifty years, many of them as its iron-fisted Speaker, he told his friends that he never expected to return to Washington.

"But if I do," he said, "it will be to walk down the Mall and stand looking up at the greatest American who ever lived."

ON A COOL, clear evening in May 1923, Henry Bacon stood on the steps of the Lincoln Memorial, the crowning achievement of a splendid life in architecture, and received from President Harding the Gold Medal of the American Institute of Architects. The seldom-awarded Gold Medal is the highest distinc-

tion that can be conferred on an American architect by his fellow architects. On February 16, 1924, after a short illness, Bacon died.

BACON'S DEATH was devastating to Daniel French. They had been close friends for thirty years as well as colleagues who understood and admired each other's talents. Bacon had even designed and built French's home and studio at Stockbridge.

In her biography of her father, Margaret French Cresson said he felt that his friend had been "lent to the world" just for the purpose of creating the Lincoln Memorial. Bacon's whole professional life had led up to that splendid accomplishment, and less than two years after the dedication of the memorial, his life was over.

Although French was seventeen years older than Bacon, he lived seven years longer, working at his beloved sculptures until his death in 1931. In the spring of 1929, French and his family returned to Washington for what he knew probably would be his last visit to the Lincoln Memorial. They made their visit on a moonlit night and paused at the foot of the great sweep of steps to look up at the glorious white temple and at the lighted figure of Lincoln inside.

After a few moments French turned to his daughter. "Margaret," he said, "I'd like to see what this will look like a thousand years from now."

A part of the First North-South Brigade, the Lancaster Fencibles of Pennsylvania, at the commemoration of President Lincoln's birthday, February 12, 1991.

Additional Information
About the Lincoln Memorial

The memorial is open to the public every day of the year, twenty-four hours a day. There is no admission charge.

The total cost of building the memorial was $2,957,000. The total cost of Lincoln's statue was $88,400.

The names of the forty-eight states in the Union at the time of the memorial's dedication in 1922 are carved on the attic walls above the frieze. A bronze tablet on the terrace leading to the memorial commemorates the addition of Alaska and Hawaii to the Union in 1959.

Since 1989 the National Park Service has held a ceremony at the memorial to commemorate the birthday of Dr. Martin Luther King, Jr. Plans are to hold the event annually on or near Dr. King's birthday, which is January 15.

A MEMORIAL FOR MR. LINCOLN

For many years the National Park Service conducted guided tours of the vast basement area beneath the memorial. Visitors could see stalactites and stalagmites which have been formed by seeping rainwater; graffiti left on the support columns by the original workmen could also be seen. The tours were halted in 1990 when asbestos was discovered in the lining of basement pipes. No information is available on when the tours may be resumed.

The pink marble sarcophagus of Robert Todd Lincoln, son of President Abraham Lincoln, stands on a shaded Arlington National Cemetery hillside, from which the Lincoln Memorial can be seen. Robert Todd Lincoln was interred at Arlington in 1926.

Since 1976, access to the Lincoln Memorial has been made easy for wheelchair-confined persons by the installation of an elevator.

Bibliography

Angle, Paul M., ed. *The Lincoln Reader.* New York: Da Capo Press, Inc., 1990. (Originally published by Greenwood Press: Westport, CT, 1947.)

Applewhite, E. J. *Washington Itself: An Informal Guide to the Capital of the United States.* New York: Alfred A. Knopf, 1981.

Cresson, Margaret French. *Journey Into Fame; The Life of Daniel Chester French.* Cambridge, MA: Harvard University Press, 1947.

Debnam, Betty. "The March on Washington." *The Washington Post* ("Mini Page"), January 13, 1991.

Freedman, Russell. *Lincoln: A Photobiography.* New York: Clarion Books, 1987.

Fry, Smith D. *Patriotic Story of the Lincoln Memorial.* Washington, D.C.: Model Printing Company, 1923.

Furbee, Leonard J. *Twenty-Four Years with Lincoln.* New York: Vantage Press, 1968.

BIBLIOGRAPHY

Gordon, Suzanne. *In This Temple: A Guide Book to the Lincoln Memorial.* Washington, D.C.: Museum Press, Inc. (in cooperation with the Parks & History Association), 1973.

Harding, Warren G. *Address at the Dedication of the Lincoln Memorial.* Washington, D.C.: Government Printing Office, 1922.

Hoig, Stan. *A Capital for the Nation.* New York: Cobblehill Books, 1990.

Jakoubek, Robert. *Martin Luther King, Jr.* New York: Chelsea House Publishers, 1989.

Kunhardt, Dorothy Meserve and Philip B. Kunhardt, Jr. *Twenty Days.* New York: Castle Books, 1965.

Lincoln Memorial. Washington, D.C.: Division of Publications, National Park Service, 1986. (Official National Park Handbook, No. 129.)

Logan, Rayford, ed. *Dictionary of American Negro Biography.* New York: W. W. Norton & Co. Inc., 1982.

Mathews, James T. *The Lincoln Memorial.* Washington, D.C.: National Art Service Co., Inc., 1934.

McPherson, James M. *Abraham Lincoln and the Second American Revolution.* New York: Oxford University Press, 1990.

Miller, Natalie. *The Story of the Lincoln Memorial.* Chicago: Children's Press, 1966.

Moton, Robert R. *Finding a Way Out: An Autobiography.* College Park, MD: McGrath Publishing Company, 1920.

Pedersen, Anne. *Kidding Around Washington, D.C.: A Young Person's Guide to the City.* Santa Fe, NM: John Muir Publications, 1989.

Richman, Michael. "Building Lincoln's Memorial." *The Washington Post,* February 13, 1984.

———. "The Long Labor of Making the Nation's Favorite Statue." *Smithsonian,* February, 1977.

Sites, Maud Kay. *The Lincoln Memorial.* Washington, D.C.: Judd & Detweiler, Inc., 1936.

St. George, Judith. *The White House: Cornerstone of a Nation.* New York: G. P. Putnam's Sons, 1990.

Trescott, Jacqueline. "Marian Anderson's Voice of Conscience." *The Washington Post,* May 3, 1991.

Washington: City and Capital. American Guide Series (Federal Writers' Project, Works Progress Administration.) Washington, D.C.: Government Printing Office, 1937.

Index

Stewart, James, 84
Stocking, Bruce, 7
Sumter High School Show Choir,
    1, 3
Sumter, South Carolina, 1, 3

Taft, Pres. (and Chief Justice)
    William Howard, 10, 30,
    73–74

Toscanini, Arturo, 84
Truman, Pres. Harry, 5

Washington Monument, 29, 34,
    35
Watseka, Illinois, 37
Whitman, Walt, 23, 26
Wilmington, North Carolina, 37
Woolsey, James, 7, 9
Wright, Frank Lloyd, 47

About the Author and the Photographer

Brent Ashabranner has written widely for young readers on American social history and complex social issues. His award-winning books include *Gavriel and Jemal: Two Boys of Jerusalem; Dark Harvest; Migrant Farmworkers in America;* and *Into a Strange Land: Unaccompanied Refugee Youth in America,* written in collaboration with his daughter Melissa.

Mr. Ashabranner spent a number of years working as an education advisor in Ethiopia, Libya, and Nigeria for the Agency for International Development. He was director of the Peace Corps in Washington, D.C. He has also lived in the Philippines and Indonesia while working for the Ford Foundation. Mr. Ashabranner now lives in Williamsburg, Virginia, where he devotes most of his time to writing.

Jennifer Ashabranner, a daughter of Brent Ashabranner, is a professional photographer whose work has appeared in many commercial publications. She has collaborated with her father on *Always to Remember: The Story of the Vietnam Veterans Memorial* and *A Grateful Nation: The Story of Arlington National Cemetery.* Ms. Ashabranner studied photography at Northern Virginia Community College and at the Smithsonian Institution in Washington, D.C.; she has supervised a photographic laboratory in a Fairfax County, Virginia, recreational program. She lives in Alexandria, Virginia.

111

Photograph Credits